KIDS THROUGHOUT HISTORY™

Kids in Colonial Times

21441

Lisa A. Wroble

The Rosen Publishing Group's
PowerKids Press™
New York

Published in 1997 by The Rosen Publishing Group, Inc.
29 East 21st Street, New York, NY 10010

First Edition

Book Design: Danielle Primiceri

Photo Credits: Cover, p. 20 © Corbis-Bettmann; pp. 4, 7, 16 © Archive Photos; pp. 8, 11, 12, 15, 19 © Bettmann.

Wroble, Lisa A.
   Kids in colonial times / Lisa A. Wroble.
       p.   cm.—(Kids throughout history)
   Includes index.
   ISBN 0-8239-5118-9
   1. United States—Social life and customs—To 1775— Juvenile literature. 2. United States—History—Colonial period, ca. 1600–1775—Juvenile literature. 3. Children—United States—History—17th century—Juvenile literature. 4. Children—United States—History—18 century—Juvenile literature. I. Title. II. Series: Wroble, Lisa A. Kids throughout history.
   E162.W93 1997
   973.2—dc21   97-803
                                                                   CIP
                                                                    AC

Manufactured in the United States of America

Contents

1   The New World   5

2   The First Colonists   6

3   Colonial Towns and Houses   9

4   Chores   10

5   Clothing   13

6   Food   14

7   Play   17

8   Religion   18

9   Education   21

10   Freedom   22

Glossary   23

Index   24

The New World

Colonial times were a period in the history of the United States that lasted from about 1607 to 1790. **Colonists** (KOL-un-ists) were people who crossed the Atlantic Ocean from England and other countries in Europe to North America—the "New World." These people set up **colonies** (KOL-un-eez), or areas where other people would come to live. The first colonists arrived in what is now called Virginia. By 1720, most of the east coast of what is now the United States was **settled** (SET-tuld) with colonial towns.

◄ *The Pilgrims were one religious group that sailed to the "New World." They founded the town of Plymouth, Massachusetts in 1620.*

The First Colonists

The colonists came to North America for many reasons. But they had one thing in common. They wanted the freedom to live the way they thought best. The first Europeans to arrive were French and Spanish **traders** (TRAY-derz). They wanted to build businesses. The next Europeans were religious groups from different countries. They felt that their beliefs were misunderstood in Europe. So they sailed 3,000 miles across the Atlantic Ocean to North America. They were looking for a new home and the freedom to practice their religions.

Colonists saw the "New World" as a place where they could live the way they wanted to. ▶

Colonial Towns and Houses

Colonial towns were simple. Most houses were made of wood and were built in rows. Each house had enough land for a vegetable garden and a pen for a few animals. Each town had a few shops, a school, and a church.

Priscilla and her family were from England. They lived in Rhode Island. Priscilla's parents, aunts, uncles, cousins, and grandparents lived together in one house. The brick fireplace was the center of family life. The fire was used to cook meals and to heat the house.

People gathered around the fireplace to talk to each other and to keep warm. This man is using a whispering tube to talk quietly to a woman sitting across the room.

Chores

Everyone had jobs to do. Priscilla's father and uncle took care of the farm animals, planted and **harvested** (HAR-ves-ted) the crops, chopped firewood, and fixed tools. Her boy cousins helped so they could learn how to do these jobs. Women and girls cooked, cleaned, and cared for the children. Priscilla made butter, soap, and candles. Her mother made clothes for the family. She spun and wove wool and linen cloth. Both kinds of cloth were dyed different colors using berries, tree bark, or walnut shells.

Everyone had chores to do. Women and girls were in charge of spinning thread to make cloth, making butter, and cooking. ▶

Clothing

The girls and women in Priscilla's family wore linen or wool dresses. Underneath, they wore **petticoats** (PET-ee-cohts). They wore white caps on their heads and leather shoes on their feet. In the winter, they wore hooded cloaks when they went outside.

Men and boys wore **breeches** (BRIT-chez), long linen shirts, and leather shoes in the summer. In the winter, they wore leather breeches, wool shirts, and heavy boots. When they went outside, they wore overcoats, leather leggings, wool mittens, and caps.

◄ *During the winter, the colonists dressed in warm clothes that the women and girls made.*

13

Food

Priscilla's family raised their own food. They grew grain, fruits, and vegetables. They raised cattle, hogs, sheep, and chickens for meat. Men also hunted deer, rabbits, and wild turkeys. They fished and collected clams from the ocean. The women made stews with the meat and vegetables. An oven was made in a wall of the fireplace. Heat from the fire baked bread and roasted meat in the oven. Corn was roasted, ground, and made into corn bread or cooked into mush.

The colonists learned how to grow corn, pumpkins, squash, and other crops from some of the Native Americans that they met. ▶

Play

Most colonists believed in a simple life of hard work. But sometimes they mixed work with play. Families gathered to build houses and barns. Men and boys held foot races and shooting contests. Women had corn husking contests and **quilting bees** (KWIL-ting BEEZ). At a quilting bee, women gathered to sew pieces of cloth into bed coverings. One quilt was made at every quilting bee. Younger children had special games, too. Priscilla and her friends played hopscotch and marbles and flew kites that they made.

◀ *Fishing was a sport that was also a way to get food.*

Religion

There were different religions in different colonies. In many colonial towns, the church was also the town hall. Church leaders had a lot of control over the way people lived. There were strict rules about how people could dress, act, and speak, especially on the Sabbath. The Sabbath was a time to think about God and to learn about what He wanted people to do. It began on Saturday afternoon and lasted until sundown on Sunday. No work could be done on the Sabbath. People couldn't even cook or make their beds!

It was important that everyone go to church on the Sabbath. ▶

Education

Teaching children was important to the colonists. Like all children, Priscilla went to school in a one-room schoolhouse. She learned to read and write. Priscilla learned to read using a **hornbook** (HORN-book). This was a piece of board with the alphabet, numbers, and a prayer printed on it. Most students learned their lessons by **memorizing** (MEM-or-eye-zing) what the teacher said. Priscilla also learned good manners and to **obey** (oh-BAY) people who were older than she was.

Colonial teachers believed that the best way for students to learn was to memorize their lessons.

Freedom

The colonists came to North America for different reasons. But they all had one thing in common. They wanted the freedom to live the way they thought best. But as the colonies grew, the king in England wanted control over the colonists. He set **taxes** (TAK-sez), or payments, on cloth, tobacco, lumber, and furs. The colonists **united** (yoo-NY-ted) to fight against these rulers. And they won. In 1776, the colonies became the United States of America. The colonists were now **citizens** (SIH-tih-zenz) of their own country.

Glossary

breeches (BRIT-chez) Loose pants that are fastened at the knee.

citizen (SIH-tih-zen) A person who is a member of a country.

colonist (KOL-un-ist) Person who moves from his own country to a new land but stays under the rule of his own country.

colony (KOL-un-ee) An area of land settled by people from another country and under the rule of that country.

harvest (HAR-vest) To gather crops.

hornbook (HORN-book) A piece of board with a handle that has the alphabet, numbers, and a prayer printed on it.

memorize (MEM-or-eyez) To learn something and be able to repeat it.

obey (oh-BAY) To do what you are told.

petticoat (PET-ee-coht) A skirt worn underneath a dress or skirt.

quilting bee (KWIL-ting BEE) A gathering of people who sew a bed covering made of layers of cloth sewn over soft padding.

settle (SET-tul) To set up house in a new place.

taxes (TAK-sez) Money or goods collected by a ruler from the people under his rule.

trader (TRAY-der) A person who exchanges goods for money or other goods.

unite (yoo-NYT) To come together.

Index

A
Atlantic Ocean, 5, 6

C
cloth, making, 10
clothing, 10, 13
colonies, 5, 18, 22
colonists, 5, 6, 21, 22
crops, 10

E
education, 21
England, 5, 9, 22
Europe, 5, 6

F
fireplace, 9, 14
food, 14
freedom, 6, 22

G
games, 17

H
hornbook, 21
houses, 9, 17

J
jobs, 10

N
"New World," 5
North America, 5, 6

Q
quilting bees, 17

R
religion, 6, 18
Rhode Island, 9

S
Sabbath, 18

T
taxes, 22
towns, 5, 9, 18

U
United States, 5, 22

V
Virginia, 5